ONE MINUTE MORNING
PREGNANCY
AFTER LOSS

GUIDED MEDITATIONS, AFFIRMATIONS
& GRATITUDE JOURNAL

THIS JOURNAL BELONGS TO:

....

YOUR FIRST THING TO BE GRATEFUL FOR, EXTRA GOODIES!
GRAB YOUR FREE GOODIES HERE:

MINDFUL PLANNER
PRESS

YOUR OMM JOURNEY

The One Minute Morning (or OMM for short) Pregnancy After Loss | Guided Meditations, Affirmations & Gratitude Journal is here to guide you in finding a way through your fears, anxiety, and feelings to begin to experience the joys of pregnancy. The magic, the miracle, the mystery - whatever you call it, you deserve to find peace, love your body again, and celebrate every milestone of this stage of your life.

This journal is separated into 4 sections: Gratitudes, Affirmations, Meditations, and Journal Pages. This book, with its meditation, affirmations, and journaling, is a form of mindfulness. The pages within offer respite from the trauma cycle that starts in your head, fueled by the past, your fears, and your anxiety. Healing starts with focusing on the present and reframing your thought patterns to see your current pregnancy.

While the book alone cannot heal you, it offers one venue for healing your aching heart and aiding you in seeing the splendor of pregnancy - of this pregnancy, of your body, and of your mind. You are a parent, your losses brought you love you'd never known and nothing can take that away. You are strong and resilient and you are here. You are pregnant and your baby is growing and you are here to see, feel, and experience it all. You owe it to yourself to delve into these pages, let yourself begin to heal, and celebrate every moment with your baby.

USING THIS OMM JOURNAL

Take a moment each morning to center yourself and meditate on gratitude or find an affirmation you connect with. Choose one of the affirmations, gratitude statements, or meditations in this journal (or pop over to the QR code to get access to the guided meditations on YouTube) and start each day with a sense of calm. The more you practice and reflect, the more you will see and feel gratitude in this pregnancy.

There are three main ways to use this journal, either go through it in order, page by page without discernment, search around for the specific page you'd like to complete that morning, or to flip to a random page each morning. There is no right or wrong way.

You also have blank lined spaces to reflect on your meditations and gratitudes, as well as blank pages for notes - a great place to add your own additional affirmations, statements of gratitude, celebration of milestones, and reflect on your feelings throughout pregnancy.

It's important to remember that healing and moving forward from a previous loss can take time and it's not a linear process. It's okay to feel a wide range of emotions and it's important to give yourself the space and time to process them. It's also important to remember that you are not alone in your journey and to reach out to friends, family, or professionals if you need support.

MEDITATION

The OMM Journal offers short guided meditations, a QR code linked to guided meditations, and reflection space for each written meditation. Learning how to meditate takes time and practice to master. These short guided meditations are a great place to start and a simple way to bring mindfulness into your daily ritual. Mindfulness and meditation go hand in hand.

Mindfulness is the act of focusing your mind and energy on the present. It allows you to quiet the mind of the to do lists and chaos of life around you. While some find it easy to quiet the mind, those who experience anxiety usually find it more difficult to hush the noise. Running thoughts interrupt the ability to meditate.

Some enjoy using something tangible to help focus on during meditation, whether it's something for your hands to fidget, a cross, coin, necklace, crystal, etc. Some use objects in meditation practice to help in channeling these thoughts and visualizing putting them inside the object. By releasing your thoughts, this aids in clearing the mind. Objects can also be used by to metaphorically carry around your affirmation of the day.

While you can use any crystal or object you connect with, some crystals that are commonly associated with meditation are white quartz, selenite, and blue agate. All offer healing and calming energy to aid in your meditation practice.

MORNING RITUAL
· MEDITATION ·

FORGIVENESS MEDITATION

CLOSE YOUR EYES AND TAKE A DEEP
BREATH IN

BRING TO MIND ANY PART OF YOU
THAT MAY BE HOLDING A GRUDGE
AGAINST YOUR BODY AND PAST
LOSSES, AND REPEAT THE WORDS "I
FORGIVE YOU"

REPEAT THE WORDS "I RELEASE THIS
GRUDGE AND LET IT GO." IMAGINE
YOURSELF FEELING LIGHTER AND
MORE AT PEACE AS YOU EXHALE

MEDITATION REFLECTION

MORNING RITUAL
·MEDITATION·

LETTING GO OF FEAR

CLOSE YOUR EYES AND TAKE A DEEP
BREATH IN

BRING TO MIND ANY FEARS OR
ANXIETIES YOU MAY HAVE ABOUT
THIS PREGNANCY OR THE FUTURE

IMAGINE A LIGHT SURROUNDING
THESE FEARS AND ANXIETIES, AND
IMAGINE YOURSELF SLOWLY LETTING
GO OF THEM AS YOU EXHALE

REPEAT THE WORDS "I LET GO OF
FEAR, I TRUST IN THE JOURNEY"

MEDITATION REFLECTION

_____

_____

_____

_____

_____

_____

MORNING RITUAL
·MEDITATION·

TRUSTING YOUR BODY MEDITATION

CLOSE YOUR EYES AND TAKE A DEEP
BREATH IN

BRING TO MIND YOUR FEARS ABOUT
YOUR BODY WORKING AGAINST YOU
AND YOUR PAST LOSSES, AND
REPEAT THE WORDS "I TRUST MY
BODY AND MY BABY TO WORK
TOGETHER"

REPEAT THE WORDS "I RELEASE MY
FEAR OF THE PAST REPEATING AND
LET IT GO." IMAGINE YOURSELF
FEELING LIGHTER AND MORE AT
PEACE AS YOU EXHALE

MEDITATION REFLECTION

MORNING RITUAL
·MEDITATION·

MINDFULNESS OF YOUR BABY'S MOVEMENTS

CLOSE YOUR EYES AND TAKE A DEEP
BREATH IN

BRING TO MIND THE SENSATION OF
YOUR BABY MOVING INSIDE OF YOU,
AND IMAGINE YOURSELF FEELING A
DEEP CONNECTION WITH YOUR BABY

REPEAT THE WORDS "I AM
CONNECTED TO MY BABY, I FEEL MY
BABY GROWING, AND MY BABY IS
HEALTHY"

MEDITATION REFLECTION

MORNING RITUAL
· M E D I T A T I O N ·

TRUSTING IN THE POWER OF CONNECTION

CLOSE YOUR EYES AND TAKE THREE DEEP BREATHS

WITH EACH BREATH, IMAGINE YOURSELF AS A NEW PARENT TO THIS NEW BABY, HOLDING YOUR BABY IN YOUR ARMS AND FEELING THE POWER OF THAT CONNECTION

REPEAT THE WORDS "I TRUST IN MY ABILITY TO BE A LOVING AND NURTURING PARENT"

MEDITATION REFLECTION

MORNING RITUAL
· M E D I T A T I O N ·

MINDFULNESS OF YOUR BABY'S HEARTBEAT

CLOSE YOUR EYES AND TAKE A DEEP
BREATH IN

BRING TO MIND THE SOUND OF YOUR
BABY'S HEARTBEAT, AND IMAGINE
YOURSELF FEELING A DEEP
CONNECTION WITH YOUR BABY

REPEAT THE WORDS "I AM
CONNECTED TO MY BABY, AND MY
BABY IS SAFE AND WELL"

MEDITATION REFLECTION

....

....

....

....

....

MORNING RITUAL
·MEDITATION·

TRUSTING IN THE PROCESS OF PREGNANCY

CLOSE YOUR EYES AND TAKE A DEEP BREATH IN

IMAGINE YOUR BABY GROWING IN YOUR BELLY, AND IMAGINE YOURSELF FEELING CALM, STRONG, AND IN CONTROL

REPEAT THE WORDS "I BELIEVE THIS BABY AND MY BODY KNOW HOW TO WORK IN UNISON TO ACHIEVE A LIVE BIRTH"

MEDITATION REFLECTION

MORNING RITUAL
· M E D I T A T I O N ·

TRUSTING IN THE JOURNEY OF PREGNANCY

CLOSE YOUR EYES AND TAKE A DEEP
BREATH IN

VISUALIZE YOUR BABY GROWING,
IMAGINE FEELING BABY KICK, SEE
YOURSELF IN LABOR, AND IMAGINE
YOURSELF FEELING CALM, STRONG,
AND IN CONTROL

REPEAT THE WORDS "I TRUST IN MY
BODY, I TRUST IN THE PROCESS, AND
I TRUST IN THE OUTCOME"

MEDITATION REFLECTION

MORNING RITUAL
· M E D I T A T I O N ·

SELF-CARE MEDITATION

CLOSE YOUR EYES AND TAKE A DEEP
BREATH IN

BRING TO MIND SOMETHING YOU
CAN DO TO TAKE CARE OF
YOURSELF, WHETHER IT'S A WARM
BATH, A WALK OUTSIDE, OR A CUP
OF TEA

REPEAT THE WORDS "I AM TAKING
CARE OF MYSELF, AND I AM WORTHY
OF LOVE AND CARE"

MEDITATION REFLECTION

MORNING RITUAL
· M E D I T A T I O N ·

MINDFULNESS OF THE PRESENT MOMENT

CLOSE YOUR EYES AND TAKE A DEEP BREATH IN

BRING TO MIND THE PRESENT MOMENT, AND FOCUS ON THE SENSATIONS, SOUNDS, AND FEELINGS YOU ARE EXPERIENCING IN THIS MOMENT

REPEAT THE WORDS "I AM HERE, I AM PRESENT, AND I AM AT PEACE"

MEDITATION REFLECTION

_____

_____

_____

_____

_____

_____

MORNING RITUAL
· M E D I T A T I O N ·

GRATITUDE FOR YOUR BABY

CLOSE YOUR EYES AND TAKE A DEEP
BREATH IN

BRING TO MIND YOUR BABY, AND
IMAGINE YOURSELF FEELING
GRATEFUL FOR THE OPPORTUNITY TO
BE A PARENT

REPEAT THE WORDS "I AM GRATEFUL
FOR MY BABY, AND I AM GRATEFUL
FOR THIS JOURNEY"

MEDITATION REFLECTION

_____

_____

_____

_____

_____

_____

MORNING RITUAL
· M E D I T A T I O N ·

BODY SCAN MEDITATION

CLOSE YOUR EYES AND TAKE A DEEP
BREATH IN

SLOWLY SCAN YOUR BODY FROM
HEAD TO TOE, NOTICING ANY AREAS
OF TENSION OR DISCOMFORT OR
FEAR

RELEASE ANY TENSION WITH EACH
EXHALE AND FOCUS ON FEELING
RELAXED AND AT EASE

MEDITATION REFLECTION

MORNING RITUAL
· M E D I T A T I O N ·

GRATITUDE MEDITATION

CLOSE YOUR EYES AND TAKE TWO
DEEP BREATHS

THINK OF SOMETHING YOU ARE
GRATEFUL FOR IN THIS MOMENT. IT
COULD BE YOUR BABY, YOUR
HEALTH, OR ANYTHING ELSE

AS YOU EXHALE, REPEAT THE WORDS
"I AM GRATEFUL FOR..."

MEDITATION REFLECTION

_____

_____

_____

_____

_____

MINDFULNESS OF BREATH MEDITATION

CLOSE YOUR EYES AND FOCUS ON YOUR BREATH

NOTICE THE SENSATION OF THE BREATH AS IT ENTERS AND EXITS YOUR BODY. REMEMBER AS YOU BREATHE IN, YOU ARE SUPPLYING OXYGEN TO YOUR BABY. YOUR BREATH IS SUSTAINING THEM

IF YOUR MIND WANDERS, GENTLY BRING IT BACK TO HOW YOUR BREATH FEELS

MEDITATION REFLECTION

_____

_____

_____

_____

_____

MORNING RITUAL
· M E D I T A T I O N ·

LOVING-KINDNESS MEDITATION

CLOSE YOUR EYES AND TAKE A DEEP
BREATH IN

BRING TO MIND YOUR BABY, AND
SILENTLY REPEAT THE WORDS "MAY
YOU BE HAPPY, MAY YOU BE
HEALTHY, MAY YOU BE AT PEACE."

THEN, BRING TO MIND YOURSELF
AND REPEAT THE WORDS "MAY I BE
HAPPY, MAY I BE HEALTHY, MAY I BE
AT PEACE."

MEDITATION REFLECTION

_____

_____

_____

_____

_____

_____

MORNING RITUAL
· M E D I T A T I O N ·

POSITIVE VISUALIZATION MEDITATION

CLOSE YOUR EYES AND TAKE A DEEP BREATH IN

IMAGINE YOURSELF HOLDING YOUR HEALTHY BABY IN YOUR ARMS, THE FEELINGS OF RELIEF, IMAGINE THE APPRECIATION YOU WILL FEEL FOR YOUR BODY, IMAGINE THE EMOTIONS YOU WILL FEEL IN THIS MOMENT

TAKE A DEEP BREATH IN, HOLD IT FOR A FEW SECONDS AND EXHALE, FEELING THE FEELING OF HAPPINESS AND GRATITUDE

MEDITATION REFLECTION

....

....

....

....

....

....

MORNING RITUAL
·MEDITATION·

RELAXATION MEDITATION

CLOSE YOUR EYES AND TAKE A DEEP
BREATH IN

SLOWLY REPEAT THE WORD "RELAX"
TO YOURSELF AS YOU EXHALE

IMAGINE EACH MUSCLE IN YOUR
BODY BECOMING MORE AND MORE
RELAXED WITH EACH BREATH

MEDITATION REFLECTION

MORNING RITUAL
· M E D I T A T I O N ·

NATURE MEDITATION

CLOSE YOUR EYES AND IMAGINE YOU
WITH YOUR BABY IN A PEACEFUL
NATURAL SETTING, LIKE A FOREST OR
A BEACH

TAKE IN THE SIGHTS, SOUNDS, AND
SENSATIONS OF THIS PLACE -
IMAGINE SHARING THIS EXPERIENCE
WITH YOUR BABY

AS YOU INHALE, IMAGINE YOURSELF
BREATHING IN PEACE AND JOY. AS
YOU EXHALE, IMAGINE YOURSELF
BREATHING OUT ANY STRESS OR
TENSION

MEDITATION REFLECTION

MORNING RITUAL
·MEDITATION·

GUIDED IMAGERY FOR BIRTH

CLOSE YOUR EYES AND IMAGINE
YOURSELF IN A PEACEFUL AND
COMFORTABLE PLACE, WITH YOUR
BABY IN YOUR ARMS

IMAGINE YOUR BODY KEEPING YOUR
BABY SAFE UNTIL BIRTH, AND
IMAGINE YOURSELF FEELING CALM,
STRONG AND IN CONTROL

IMAGINE YOURSELF HOLDING YOUR
BABY IN YOUR HOME, FEELING THE
ELATION AND LOVE OF THIS MOMENT

MEDITATION REFLECTION

SELF-COMPASSION MEDITATION

CLOSE YOUR EYES AND TAKE A DEEP
BREATH IN

LET YOUR FEELINGS AROUND YOUR
LOSS(ES) COME TO MIND, FOCUS ON
YOU MOVING THROUGH THE
PROCESS OF HEALING AND REPEAT
THE WORDS "I AM STRUGGLING AND
THAT'S OKAY."

REPEAT THE WORDS "MAY I BE KIND
TO MYSELF, MAY I BE PATIENT WITH
MYSELF, MAY I ACCEPT MYSELF AS I
AM."

MEDITATION REFLECTION

_____

_____

_____

_____

_____

_____

MORNING RITUAL
·MEDITATION·

TRUSTING THE JOURNEY

CLOSE YOUR EYES AND TAKE A DEEP
BREATH IN

IMAGINE A PATH OR A ROAD AHEAD
OF YOU, AND IMAGINE YOURSELF
WALKING ON THIS PATH, KNOWING
THAT IT'S TAKING YOU AND YOUR
BABY TOWARD GOING HOME
TOGETHER, SAFE AND HEALTHY

IMAGINE YOURSELF FEELING CALM
AND AT PEACE, KNOWING THAT
EVERYTHING IS WORKING TOWARD
THIS GOAL

MEDITATION REFLECTION

MORNING RITUAL
· M E D I T A T I O N ·

MINDFULNESS OF YOUR BABY

CLOSE YOUR EYES AND TAKE A DEEP
BREATH IN

FOCUS YOUR ATTENTION ON YOUR
BABY, AND IMAGINE YOURSELF
FEELING THE MOVEMENTS OF YOUR
BABY

VISUALIZE YOUR CONNECTION WITH
YOUR BABY, AND TAKE A FEW DEEP
BREATHS IN AND OUT, FEELING THE
LOVE AND CONNECTION WITH YOUR
BABY

MEDITATION REFLECTION

....

....

....

....

....

MORNING RITUAL
· A F F I R M A T I O N ·

I AM CAPABLE OF HEALING AND
MOVING FORWARD FROM MY
PREVIOUS LOSS

AFFIRMATION REFLECTION

_____

_____

_____

_____

_____

_____

MORNING RITUAL
· A F F I R M A T I O N ·

I AM CONFIDENT IN MY ABILITY TO PROVIDE LOVE AND CARE FOR MY FAMILY

AFFIRMATION REFLECTION

_____

_____

_____

_____

_____

_____

MORNING RITUAL
· A F F I R M A T I O N ·

I AM CONFIDENT IN MY ABILITY TO BE
A GREAT PARENT

AFFIRMATION REFLECTION

_____

_____

_____

_____

_____

_____

MORNING RITUAL
·AFFIRMATION·

I AM CAPABLE OF HEALING AND
CELEBRATING MY BODY

AFFIRMATION REFLECTION

_____

_____

_____

_____

_____

_____

MORNING RITUAL
·AFFIRMATION·

I AM FILLED WITH HOPE AND PROMISE FOR A TAKE HOME BABY

AFFIRMATION REFLECTION

MORNING RITUAL
· A F F I R M A T I O N ·

I AM SURROUNDED BY LOVE AND
POSITIVITY AS I LEARN TO
APPRECIATE MY BODY

AFFIRMATION REFLECTION

MORNING RITUAL
· A F F I R M A T I O N ·

I TRUST IN THE POWER OF MY MIND
DURING THIS PREGNANCY

AFFIRMATION REFLECTION

I CHOOSE TO RELEASE ANY NEGATIVE THOUGHTS ABOUT THIS PREGNANCY

AFFIRMATION REFLECTION

_____

_____

_____

_____

_____

_____

MORNING RITUAL
· A F F I R M A T I O N ·

I AM STRONG AND CAPABLE OF
HANDLING ANY CHALLENGES THAT
MAY COME WITH THIS PREGNANCY

AFFIRMATION REFLECTION

MORNING RITUAL
·AFFIRMATION·

I FEEL LOVE AND POSITIVITY TOWARD
MY BODY AND PREGNANCY

AFFIRMATION REFLECTION

_____

_____

_____

_____

_____

_____

MORNING RITUAL
·AFFIRMATION·

I LOVE MY BABY

AFFIRMATION REFLECTION

MORNING RITUAL
· A F F I R M A T I O N ·

I AM CONFIDENT IN MY ABILITY TO
PROVIDE LOVE AND CARE FOR MY
BABY

AFFIRMATION REFLECTION

MORNING RITUAL
·AFFIRMATION·

I AM STRONG AND RESILIENT

AFFIRMATION REFLECTION

_____

_____

_____

_____

_____

_____

I TRUST IN THE INNATE KNOWLEDGE
OF THE HUMAN BODY

AFFIRMATION REFLECTION

....

....

....

....

....

....

MORNING RITUAL
·AFFIRMATION·

I CHOOSE TO RELEASE ANY NEGATIVE
THOUGHTS ABOUT MY BODY
CARRYING A BABY TO TERM

AFFIRMATION REFLECTION

MORNING RITUAL
·AFFIRMATION·

I RELEASE MY FEAR AND TRUST IN THE
JOURNEY OF THIS PREGNANCY

AFFIRMATION REFLECTION

_____

_____

_____

_____

_____

_____

MORNING RITUAL
·AFFIRMATION·

I SEE THE BEAUTY IN EVERY MOMENT
WITH THIS BABY

AFFIRMATION REFLECTION

MORNING RITUAL
·AFFIRMATION·

I CHOOSE TO MOVE MY BODY IN WAYS THAT FEEL GOOD

AFFIRMATION REFLECTION

MORNING RITUAL
·AFFIRMATION·

I AM FILLED WITH HOPE AND PROMISE FOR A HEALTHY BABY AND BIRTH

AFFIRMATION REFLECTION

MORNING RITUAL
·AFFIRMATION·

I AM FILLED WITH HOPE AND
EXCITEMENT FOR THE FUTURE WITH
MY BABY

AFFIRMATION REFLECTION

....

....

....

....

....

....

MORNING RITUAL
·AFFIRMATION·

I AM FILLED WITH JOY AND WONDER
AS I WATCH MY BABY GROW AND
DEVELOP

AFFIRMATION REFLECTION

MORNING RITUAL
·AFFIRMATION·

I CHOOSE TO FOCUS ON THE
PRESENT MOMENT AND ENJOY THIS
MOMENT WITH MY BABY

AFFIRMATION REFLECTION

MORNING RITUAL
·AFFIRMATION·

I AM OPEN TO THE LOVE AND BOND
THAT IS GROWING BETWEEN ME AND
MY BABY

AFFIRMATION REFLECTION

MORNING RITUAL
·AFFIRMATION·

I AM SURROUNDED BY A COMMUNITY
WHO UNDERSTANDS AND SUPPORTS
ME

AFFIRMATION REFLECTION

_____

_____

_____

_____

_____

_____

MORNING RITUAL
·AFFIRMATION·

I AM CONFIDENT IN MY ABILITY TO PROVIDE LOVE AND CARE FOR MY BODY

AFFIRMATION REFLECTION

_____

_____

_____

_____

_____

_____

MORNING RITUAL
·AFFIRMATION·

I AM LEARNING TO APPRECIATE MY RESILIENCE AND STRENGTH ON THIS JOURNEY

AFFIRMATION REFLECTION

_____

_____

_____

_____

_____

_____

MORNING RITUAL
· A F F I R M A T I O N ·

I TRUST IN THE GUIDANCE AND SUPPORT OF MY HEALTHCARE TEAM

AFFIRMATION REFLECTION

MORNING RITUAL
·AFFIRMATION·

I TRUST THAT MY BODY IS DOING
EVERYTHING IT CAN TO KEEP MY
BABY SAFE

AFFIRMATION REFLECTION

MORNING RITUAL
·AFFIRMATION·

I BELIEVE THAT MY INTUITION CAN BE
REMINDED OF MY BODY'S STRENGTH

AFFIRMATION REFLECTION

MORNING RITUAL
·AFFIRMATION·

I CHOOSE TO FOCUS ON THE PRESENT AND NOT WORRY ABOUT THE FUTURE

AFFIRMATION REFLECTION

MORNING RITUAL
·AFFIRMATION·

I TRUST IN THE JOURNEY AND WILL
WATCH IN AWE AS MY BODY
NURTURES MY BABY

AFFIRMATION REFLECTION

MORNING RITUAL
·AFFIRMATION·

I CHOOSE TO LET GO OF FEAR AND
EMBRACE THE BEAUTY OF THIS
PREGNANCY

AFFIRMATION REFLECTION

MORNING RITUAL
· A F F I R M A T I O N ·

I AM SURROUNDED BY LOVE AND
SUPPORT FROM MY FAMILY AND
FRIENDS

AFFIRMATION REFLECTION

MORNING RITUAL
· A F F I R M A T I O N ·

I CHOOSE TO HONOR ALL MY BODY
HAS OVERCOME TO GET US HERE

AFFIRMATION REFLECTION

MORNING RITUAL
·AFFIRMATION·

I TRUST IN THE POWER OF HEALING DURING THIS PREGNANCY

AFFIRMATION REFLECTION

MORNING RITUAL
·AFFIRMATION·

I CHOOSE TO LET GO OF FEAR AND
EMBRACE THE CHANGES THAT ARE
HAPPENING TO MY BODY

AFFIRMATION REFLECTION

MORNING RITUAL
·AFFIRMATION·

I AM LEARNING TO MEET EACH FEARFUL MOMENT WITH DEEP BREATHS

AFFIRMATION REFLECTION

_____

_____

_____

_____

_____

MORNING RITUAL
·AFFIRMATION·

I CHOOSE TO FOCUS ON THE
PRESENT AND NOT LET MY FEAR
OVERCOME THE JOY OF THIS
PREGNANCY

AFFIRMATION REFLECTION

MORNING RITUAL
·AFFIRMATION·

I APPRECIATE HOW HARD MY BABY
AND BODY ARE WORKING TOGETHER

AFFIRMATION REFLECTION

I AM REMINDING MYSELF THAT MY
MIND IS CAPABLE OF HEALING

AFFIRMATION REFLECTION

_____

_____

_____

_____

_____

_____

MORNING RITUAL
·AFFIRMATION·

I AM SURROUNDED BY HOPE DURING
THIS PREGNANCY

AFFIRMATION REFLECTION

MORNING RITUAL
· A F F I R M A T I O N ·

I TRUST THAT I WILL MEET EACH MOMENT WITH CALMNESS

AFFIRMATION REFLECTION

_____

_____

_____

_____

_____

_____

MORNING RITUAL
· A F F I R M A T I O N ·

I AM SURROUNDED BY LOVE AND SUPPORT FROM MY VILLAGE

AFFIRMATION REFLECTION

I AM REMINDING MYSELF THAT THIS BABY IS DIFFERENT

AFFIRMATION REFLECTION

MORNING RITUAL
·AFFIRMATION·

I AM FILLED WITH HOPE AND
EXCITEMENT FOR THE FUTURE

AFFIRMATION REFLECTION

MORNING RITUAL
·AFFIRMATION·

I CHOOSE TO FOCUS ON THE POSITIVE ASPECTS OF THIS PREGNANCY AND NOT DWELL ON THE PAST

AFFIRMATION REFLECTION

_____

_____

_____

_____

_____

MORNING RITUAL
·AFFIRMATION·

I AM REMINDING MYSELF THAT MY BODY IS CAPABLE OF HEALING

AFFIRMATION REFLECTION

_____

_____

_____

_____

_____

_____

MORNING RITUAL
·AFFIRMATION·

I AM POSITIVE ABOUT THIS
PREGNANCY

AFFIRMATION REFLECTION

MORNING RITUAL
· A F F I R M A T I O N ·

I TRUST IN THE POWER OF MY BODY
DURING THIS PREGNANCY

AFFIRMATION REFLECTION

MORNING RITUAL
·AFFIRMATION·

I AM FILLED WITH HOPE AND
EXCITEMENT FOR THE FUTURE VISION
OF MY FAMILY

AFFIRMATION REFLECTION

_____

_____

_____

_____

_____

_____

MORNING RITUAL
·AFFIRMATION·

I CHOOSE TO FOCUS ON THE PRESENT AND WHAT MY BODY IS DOING NOW

AFFIRMATION REFLECTION

MORNING RITUAL
· A F F I R M A T I O N ·

I AM FILLED WITH HOPE AND
GRATITUDE FOR THE WORK MY BODY
HAS DONE TO GET US HERE

AFFIRMATION REFLECTION

MORNING RITUAL
·AFFIRMATION·

I AM CONFIDENT IN THE LOVE AND
BOND THAT I HAVE WITH MY BABY

AFFIRMATION REFLECTION

_____

_____

_____

_____

_____

_____

MORNING RITUAL
· A F F I R M A T I O N ·

I TRUST IN MY ABILITY TO BE A
LOVING AND NURTURING PARENT

AFFIRMATION REFLECTION

_____

_____

_____

_____

_____

MORNING RITUAL
· AFFIRMATION ·

I AM REMINDING MYSELF DAILY THAT
THIS PREGNANCY IS NEW

AFFIRMATION REFLECTION

_____

_____

_____

_____

_____

_____

MORNING RITUAL
· A F F I R M A T I O N ·

I CHOOSE TO LET GO OF FEAR AND
FACE EACH STEP AS THEY COME

AFFIRMATION REFLECTION

_____

_____

_____

_____

_____

_____

MORNING RITUAL
·AFFIRMATION·

I TRUST IN MY BODY'S ABILITY TO CARRY THIS BABY TO TERM

AFFIRMATION REFLECTION

I CHOOSE TO SEE THE BEAUTY IN
THIS PREGNANCY AND NOT FOCUS
ON MY FEARS AND ANXIETY

AFFIRMATION REFLECTION

MORNING RITUAL
·AFFIRMATION·

I AM FILLED WITH HOPE AND PROMISE FOR THIS RAINBOW BABY

AFFIRMATION REFLECTION

MORNING RITUAL
·AFFIRMATION·

I LOVE MY BODY

AFFIRMATION REFLECTION

_____

_____

_____

_____

_____

_____

MORNING RITUAL
· A F F I R M A T I O N ·

I TRUST IN THE PROCESS OF PREGNANCY AND BIRTH

AFFIRMATION REFLECTION

_____

_____

_____

_____

_____

MORNING RITUAL
·AFFIRMATION·

I AM FILLED WITH HOPE AND
EXCITEMENT FOR EACH MILESTONE
THIS PREGNANCY ACHIEVES

AFFIRMATION REFLECTION

MORNING RITUAL
· A F F I R M A T I O N ·

I AM FILLED WITH JOY AND
GRATITUDE FOR THIS NEW LIFE
GROWING INSIDE OF ME

AFFIRMATION REFLECTION

MORNING RITUAL
·AFFIRMATION·

I TRUST IN THE POWER OF POSITIVITY AND OPTIMISM DURING THIS PREGNANCY

AFFIRMATION REFLECTION

MORNING RITUAL
· AFFIRMATION ·

I AM SURROUNDED BY LOVE AND
POSITIVITY AS I NAVIGATE THIS
PREGNANCY

AFFIRMATION REFLECTION

_____

_____

_____

_____

_____

MORNING RITUAL
·GRATITUDE·

I HONOR MY MIND, MY BODY,
AND MY SPIRIT FOR WORKING
TOGETHER TO HEAL AFTER
MY LOSS(ES)

GRATITUDE REFLECTION

....

....

....

....

....

....

MORNING RITUAL
· GRATITUDE ·

I AM GRATEFUL FOR THE
HOPE THAT THIS
PREGNANCY BRINGS FOR
THE FUTURE

GRATITUDE REFLECTION

....

....

....

....

....

MORNING RITUAL
·GRATITUDE·

I LOOK FORWARD TO
BIRTHING MY BABY, HOLDING
MY BABY, AND TAKING MY
BABY HOME WITH ME

GRATITUDE REFLECTION

_____

_____

_____

_____

_____

MORNING RITUAL
· G R A T I T U D E ·

I AM GRATEFUL FOR THE
CHANCE TO CREATE A NEW
CHAPTER IN MY LIFE

GRATITUDE REFLECTION

MORNING RITUAL
· GRATITUDE ·

I AM GRATEFUL FOR THE STRENGTH AND RESILIENCE OF MY BODY

GRATITUDE REFLECTION

_____

_____

_____

_____

_____

_____

MORNING RITUAL
·GRATITUDE·

I AM GRATEFUL FOR
MINDFULNESS GIVING ME
THE ABILITY TO FOCUS ON
THE PRESENT AND NOT
WORRY ABOUT THE FUTURE

GRATITUDE REFLECTION

MORNING RITUAL
·GRATITUDE·

I AM GRATEFUL FOR THE OPPORTUNITY TO GROW LIFE AGAIN

GRATITUDE REFLECTION

_____

_____

_____

_____

_____

_____

MORNING RITUAL
· G R A T I T U D E ·

I AM GRATEFUL FOR THE JOY OF FEELING MY BABY GROW AND DEVELOP

GRATITUDE REFLECTION

_____

_____

_____

_____

_____

MORNING RITUAL
·GRATITUDE·

I AM GRATEFUL FOR THE
HOPE AND JOY THIS
PREGNANCY BRINGS ME

GRATITUDE REFLECTION

_____

_____

_____

_____

_____

_____

MORNING RITUAL
· G R A T I T U D E ·

I AM GRATEFUL FOR THE
ABILITY TO TRUST IN THE
JOURNEY AND THE
OUTCOME

GRATITUDE REFLECTION

I AM GRATEFUL FOR THE
HOPE AND PROMISE OF A
NEW LIFE

GRATITUDE REFLECTION

_____

_____

_____

_____

_____

_____

MORNING RITUAL
· GRATITUDE ·

I AM GRATEFUL FOR MY PERSEVERANCE

GRATITUDE REFLECTION

_____

_____

_____

_____

_____

MORNING RITUAL
·GRATITUDE·

I AM GRATEFUL FOR MY HEALTHCARE TEAM AND THEIR CARE AND SUPPORT

GRATITUDE REFLECTION

_____

_____

_____

_____

_____

_____

MORNING RITUAL
·GRATITUDE·

I AM GRATEFUL FOR THE
HOPE AND PROMISE OF A
NEW PREGNANCY

GRATITUDE REFLECTION

_____

_____

_____

_____

_____

_____

I AM GRATEFUL FOR THE
ABILITY TO APPRECIATE EACH
DAY AND EACH MILESTONE
OF THIS PREGNANCY

GRATITUDE REFLECTION

_____

_____

_____

_____

_____

MORNING RITUAL
·GRATITUDE·

I AM GRATEFUL FOR THE
CHANCE TO MAKE THIS
PREGNANCY A SUCCESS

GRATITUDE REFLECTION

_____

_____

_____

_____

_____

_____

MORNING RITUAL
·GRATITUDE·

I AM GRATEFUL FOR THE LOVE AND SUPPORT OF MY FAMILY AND FRIENDS

GRATITUDE REFLECTION

_____

_____

_____

_____

_____

MORNING RITUAL
·GRATITUDE·

I AM GRATEFUL FOR THE
CHANCE TO EXPERIENCING
HEALING THROUGH THIS
PREGNANCY AND JOURNAL

GRATITUDE REFLECTION

MORNING RITUAL
·GRATITUDE·

I AM GRATEFUL FOR THE
OPPORTUNITY TO GIVE MY
BABY A LOVING HOME AND
FAMILY

GRATITUDE REFLECTION

MORNING RITUAL
·GRATITUDE·

I AM GRATEFUL FOR THE
POWER OF POSITIVITY,
GRATITUDE, AND HEALING
IN MY LIFE

GRATITUDE REFLECTION

_____

_____

_____

_____

_____

MORNING RITUAL
·GRATITUDE·

I AM GRATEFUL FOR THE
CHANCE TO CREATE NEW
MEMORIES AND MOVE
FORWARD

GRATITUDE REFLECTION

_____

_____

_____

_____

_____

_____

MORNING RITUAL
·GRATITUDE·

I AM GRATEFUL FOR THE
KNOWLEDGE AND
GUIDANCE OF MY
HEALTHCARE TEAM

GRATITUDE REFLECTION

_____

_____

_____

_____

_____

MORNING RITUAL
·GRATITUDE·

I AM GRATEFUL FOR THE
MOMENTS OF PEACE AND
CONTENTMENT I FEEL
DURING THIS PREGNANCY

GRATITUDE REFLECTION

_____

_____

_____

_____

_____

_____

MORNING RITUAL
·GRATITUDE·

I AM GRATEFUL FOR THE
ABILITY TO APPRECIATE THE
SMALL MOMENTS OF JOY
DURING THIS PREGNANCY

GRATITUDE REFLECTION

_____

_____

_____

_____

_____

MORNING RITUAL
·GRATITUDE·

I AM GRATEFUL FOR THE CHANCE TO BOND WITH MY BABY DURING THIS PREGNANCY

GRATITUDE REFLECTION

_____

_____

_____

_____

_____

I AM GRATEFUL FOR THE CHANCE TO BOND WITH MYSELF DURING THIS PREGNANCY

GRATITUDE REFLECTION

MORNING RITUAL
·GRATITUDE·

I AM GRATEFUL FOR THE JOY
AND EXCITEMENT OF FEELING
MY BABY MOVE

GRATITUDE REFLECTION

_____

_____

_____

_____

_____

_____

MORNING RITUAL
·GRATITUDE·

I AM GRATEFUL FOR THE
ABILITY TO FIND STRENGTH
AND COURAGE IN THE FACE
OF UNCERTAINTY

GRATITUDE REFLECTION

I AM GRATEFUL FOR THE
CHANCE TO HEAL AND MOVE
FORWARD FROM MY
PREVIOUS LOSS(ES)

GRATITUDE REFLECTION

MORNING RITUAL
·GRATITUDE·

I AM GRATEFUL FOR THE ABILITY TO SEE THE BEAUTY AND WONDER IN THIS PREGNANCY

GRATITUDE REFLECTION

_____

_____

_____

_____

_____

_____

MORNING RITUAL
·GRATITUDE·

I AM GRATEFUL FOR THE
SUPPORT AND
ENCOURAGEMENT OF MY
LOVED ONES

GRATITUDE REFLECTION

_____

_____

_____

_____

_____

_____

MORNING RITUAL
·GRATITUDE·

I AM GRATEFUL FOR THE AWARENESS THAT MY BODY KNOWS HOW TO WORK IN CONCERT WITH MY BABY

GRATITUDE REFLECTION

I AM GRATEFUL FOR THE
HOPE THAT THIS PREGNANCY
BRINGS FOR THE FUTURE

GRATITUDE REFLECTION

....

....

....

....

....

MORNING RITUAL
·GRATITUDE·

I AM GRATEFUL THAT MY
BABY IS ON THEIR WAY TO
COMING HOME WITH ME

GRATITUDE REFLECTION

MORNING RITUAL
·GRATITUDE·

I AM GRATEFUL FOR THE
OPPORTUNITY TO GIVE MY
BABY THE BEST POSSIBLE
START IN LIFE

GRATITUDE REFLECTION

_____

_____

_____

_____

_____

_____

MORNING RITUAL
·GRATITUDE·

I AM GRATEFUL FOR THE MY BODY'S HARDWORK DURING PREGNANCY

GRATITUDE REFLECTION

I AM GRATEFUL FOR THE
COMMUNITY OF OTHERS
WHO HAVE EXPERIENCED
LOSS AND UNDERSTAND MY
JOURNEY

GRATITUDE REFLECTION

_____

_____

_____

_____

_____

_____

MORNING RITUAL
·GRATITUDE·

I AM GRATEFUL FOR THE
AWARENESS THAT THIS
PREGNANCY IS NEW TO MY
BODY - A NEW LINING, A
NEW PLACENTA, A NEW
AMNIOTIC SAC

GRATITUDE REFLECTION

I AM GRATEFUL FOR THE
LOVE AND SUPPORT OF MY
VILLAGE DURING THIS
DIFFICULT TIME

GRATITUDE REFLECTION

_____

_____

_____

_____

_____

_____

MORNING RITUAL
·GRATITUDE·

I AM GRATEFUL THAT MY
BODY IS STRONG AND
CAPABLE

GRATITUDE REFLECTION

I AM GRATEFUL FOR THE
CHANCE TO CREATE A NEW
STORY FOR MY FAMILY

GRATITUDE REFLECTION

_____

_____

_____

_____

_____

_____

MORNING RITUAL
·GRATITUDE·

I AM GRATEFUL THAT MY
BODY IS READY FOR MY
BABY

GRATITUDE REFLECTION

_____

_____

_____

_____

_____

MORNING RITUAL
· G R A T I T U D E ·

I AM GRATEFUL FOR THE
KNOWLEDGE THAT I AM NOT
ALONE IN THIS JOURNEY

GRATITUDE REFLECTION

_____

_____

_____

_____

_____

MORNING RITUAL
·GRATITUDE·

I AM GRATEFUL THAT MY
BODY IS PREPARING MY
BABY FOR BEING EARTHSIDE

GRATITUDE REFLECTION

_____

_____

_____

_____

_____

MORNING RITUAL
·GRATITUDE·

I AM GRATEFUL FOR THE CHANCE TO EXPERIENCE THE MIRACLE OF PREGNANCY AGAIN

GRATITUDE REFLECTION

_____

_____

_____

_____

_____

MORNING RITUAL
·GRATITUDE·

I AM GRATEFUL FOR THE
ABILITY TO BE PRESENT
AND ENJOY EACH MOMENT
OF THIS PREGNANCY

GRATITUDE REFLECTION

_____

_____

_____

_____

_____

MORNING RITUAL
·GRATITUDE·

I AM GRATEFUL FOR THE JOY
OF WATCHING MY BABY
GROW AND DEVELOP

GRATITUDE REFLECTION

_____

_____

_____

_____

_____

MORNING RITUAL
· GRATITUDE ·

I AM GRATEFUL FOR THE KNOWLEDGE THAT THIS IS A DIFFERENT PREGNANCY

GRATITUDE REFLECTION

....

....

....

....

....

I AM GRATEFUL FOR THE ADVANCEMENTS IN MEDICAL TECHNOLOGY THAT GIVE ME PEACE OF MIND

GRATITUDE REFLECTION

_____

_____

_____

_____

_____

MORNING RITUAL
· G R A T I T U D E ·

I BELIEVE MY BODY WANTS
TO WORK WITH ME TO
BRING MY BABY HOME TO
ME

GRATITUDE REFLECTION

....

....

....

....

....

MORNING RITUAL
·GRATITUDE·

I AM GRATEFUL FOR THE
ABILITY TO TRUST IN MY
BODY'S ABILITY TO CARRY
THIS BABY TO TERM

GRATITUDE REFLECTION

....

....

....

....

....

....

MORNING RITUAL
·JOURNAL·

DATE

DATE ....

MORNING RITUAL
· JOURNAL ·

MORNING RITUAL

·JOURNAL·

DATE _____

_____

_____

_____

_____

_____

_____

_____

_____

_____

_____

_____

_____

_____

_____

_____

_____

_____

_____

_____

_____

_____

MORNING RITUAL
·JOURNAL·

MORNING RITUAL
·JOURNAL·

DATE

MORNING RITUAL
· JOURNAL ·

MORNING RITUAL
·JOURNAL·

DATE

MORNING RITUAL
· JOURNAL ·

MORNING RITUAL
· J O U R N A L ·

DATE ....

....

....

....

....

....

....

....

....

....

....

....

....

....

....

....

....

....

....

....

....

....

....

....

MORNING RITUAL
· JOURNAL ·

MORNING RITUAL
·JOURNAL·

DATE

MORNING RITUAL
· JOURNAL ·

MORNING RITUAL

· J O U R N A L ·

DATE _____

_____

_____

_____

_____

_____

_____

_____

_____

_____

_____

_____

_____

_____

_____

_____

_____

_____

_____

_____

_____

_____

DATE _____

MORNING RITUAL
· JOURNAL ·

MORNING RITUAL
·JOURNAL·

DATE _____

MORNING RITUAL
·JOURNAL·

MORNING RITUAL
·JOURNAL·

DATE

DATE

MORNING RITUAL
·JOURNAL·

MORNING RITUAL
·JOURNAL·

DATE

MORNING RITUAL
· J O U R N A L ·

MORNING RITUAL
· J O U R N A L ·

DATE ....

DATE _____

MORNING RITUAL
·JOURNAL·

_____
_____
_____
_____
_____
_____
_____
_____
_____
_____
_____
_____
_____
_____
_____
_____
_____
_____
_____
_____
_____
_____
_____

MORNING RITUAL
· JOURNAL ·

DATE _____

_____

_____

_____

_____

_____

_____

_____

_____

_____

_____

_____

_____

_____

_____

_____

_____

_____

_____

_____

_____

_____

_____

_____

MORNING RITUAL
· J O U R N A L ·

Made in the USA
Monee, IL
09 March 2023

29501278R00092